RELE
HURT AND
SADNESS

BY LIZ ADAMSON

THE ULTIMATE GUIDES
TO EMOTIONAL FREEDOM.

Releasing Hurt and Sadness

Published by Diviniti publishing Ltd.
6, Elm Walk, Aylesford, Kent.
Tel: 01622 792866

1st Edition.

Printed in Hong Kong

ISBN 1 901923 45 2

HURT AND SADNESS

Hurt and sadness are at the base of most of our negative emotions. Consequently they need to be addressed if we are to be free of the constraints of our destructive feelings. Many of our fears are about being emotionally or physically hurt. Our anger is usually a cover for our hurt. There is also a great deal of pain behind guilt, jealousy and resentment.

Our society does not tolerate the expression or demonstration of our deep feelings. We will often ridicule or shame people for showing their pain and sadness. The reason for this is that we may fear that other people's pain will touch into our own and bring these carefully suppressed feelings to the surface. Many people go through life avoiding any situation that might trigger their hurt.

When our pain is suppressed, it will seriously affect many areas of our lives. The main ones of these are relationships, friendships, family and our ability to parent successfully.

It is essential that we address the issue of our hurt and pain. It is perfectly possible to release all of our sadness without having it disrupt and affect our whole existence. When we allow this to happen, we create the freedom to love and give of ourselves without restraint. The rewards for this are unlimited.

WHAT IS HURT?

WE EXPERIENCE HURT AND PAIN WHEN WE CHOOSE TO PERCEIVE THE ACTIONS OR WORDS OF OTHERS TO HAVE A NEGATIVE EFFECT ON US.

Hurt is always a **CHOICE**. However, it may be an unconscious one. We could put two people in exactly the same situation and one may feel hurt, while the other may not have perceived any reason to feel it.

The degree of hurt that we feel will usually depend on our sensitivity. The more sensitive we are the deeper we feel things and therefore the more acute our pain will be. Many people choose to desensitise themselves as a means of protection. This decision can be very destructive because when we disconnect from our hurt we may not be aware of how we inflict hurt on others.

We are made to feel that sensitivity is not a good thing to have. We may be accused of being too sensitive. Society values reason and logic over feelings and emotions. The reality is that sensitivity is a huge gift that in adulthood can be used to great effect. Feelings are the language of the soul. They are the hot line to our intuition and guidance. Sensitivity in childhood can seem to be more of a curse than a gift. We experience everything that happens to us and around us through our feelings. If these circumstances are negative or involve struggle and strife, then the feelings created will also be negative.

HURT AND SEPARATION

Virtually all the hurt we experience is due to separation and loss. The greatest hurt we may feel is with the loss of a loved one. However, there are many more subtle causes of hurt.

Some of these are:
Hurt from abandonment.
Hurt from rejection.
Hurt from not getting our needs met.
Hurt from powerlessness.
Hurt from indifference.
Hurt from lack of love.
Hurt from being controlled.
Hurt from criticism and judgements.
Hurt from lack of communication.
Hurt at being taken for granted.

Hurt is always an illusion. We choose to perceive the actions of others as being hurtful. We in effect give them the power to hurt us. In reality, at our deepest core level there is **NO** separation. What appears to separate us is simply old patterns and damage that are illusions anyway.

Separation occurs when we disconnect from our true self. This usually happens when we are very young and when fear obscures our inner light. From this point on we experience separation as the norm, little realising that this does not exist in reality. When we reconnect with our true selves, we will never feel hurt or sadness again.

Healing the pain of separation is one of the most important aspects of freeing ourselves from hurt.

HURT AND THE EGO

There are two opposing inner aspects of ourselves that determine how we perceive or react to a situation. Our **DIVINE** aspect knows only love and its by-products. It will only see good and opportunity in every situation. The ego on the other hand works with fear and will find the negative in anything we experience.

When we have hurt and pain, it occurs because we have allowed our ego to perceive the situation.

HURT IS ALWAYS AN ILLUSION. WHEN WE CHOOSE TO PERCEIVE OURSELVES TO BE HURT, WE APPEAR TO CREATE THAT REALITY.

The ego will tell us that we are not getting our needs met because we are not loved or wanted, not good enough or not worthy. Once this perception is lodged in the unconscious mind, we will attract people and situations that reinforce these beliefs. We then react to each of these with hurt, pain and sadness. Once these patterns are firmly entrenched, it may be hard to dislodge them and see them for the illusion that they are.

The ego will also use our fear of being hurt as a way of controlling us and our actions. If we are doing something new or adventurous, we might be told that we would be hurt if we take that particular course of action. This may be enough to stop us and our lives will be severely limited. For instance if we are hurt by rejection but we want to get a new job, our ego might persuade us not to put in an application for any jobs advertised in case we are rejected and we will then experience the hurt that we are trying to avoid.

The ego has a very important positive part to play in our lives. It will show us at various points in our lives, all the unhealed hurt that we have from the past. If we use this information to consciously release our old hurts and illusions, we can eventually be completely free from emotional pain.

HURT AND THE CHILD

The source of virtually **ALL** our hurt and pain is in childhood. Patterns that are created in the first seven years of life will often repeat again and again as we get older. The pain experienced in each repetition of the pattern will also increase. We tend to attract to us people and situations that fit our particular patterning. For instance if we were abandoned by a parent as a baby or small child, we would experience a great deal of hurt. We might then go through life having friends and lovers who also abandon us. We might even unconsciously decide to avoid having friends and lovers in order not to experience the pain. We will end up feeling it anyway, we may feel abandoned because we don't have friends and lovers. Another scenario that may occur is that we are popular and in good relationships but our **FEAR** of abandonment will mean that we believe that these people might leave us. Even if this does not happen, the fear is often worse than the reality.

When we are babies and children, we are totally in our **FEELING** mode. We experience our emotions very deeply and we may be hypersensitive. Our ability to rationalise and reason develops later in life. Consequently we may feel a great deal of hurt at the tiniest of incidents that to any adult would hardly be noticed. We may also be very empathic when we are young, we pick up on the feelings and experiences of those around us and take them on as if they are our own. This can even occur in the womb. I have a friend whose mother died when she was pregnant with her second child. The child was clearly affected by her mother's grief and cries constantly.

When we are able to cry, not only do we release the pain, but also we usually get the cuddle, reassurance or attention that was needed in the first place. When this occurs there is no need to hold onto the hurt. Most of the pain that we feel in childhood will be as a result of not getting our needs and desires met. The pain only becomes stored in the body when we express the feeling but it does **NOT** create the desired outcome **OR** when we are unable to express our hurt at the time. This may be because we have been given the message that our crying meets with a negative response. There may also be cases where we decide to protect the other person from our pain.

In order to remove and release our pain, it may be necessary to go back to the incidents in childhood that have created it. These may be compounded many times over by the repetition of these patterns in our lives.

When we take note of what triggers our hurt and pain and have a willingness to go back and heal the source of it, then we can begin to eliminate sadness from our lives.

SIGNS THAT HURT IS AN ISSUE

When we have a great deal of hurt inside, we will often look for ways not to experience it. Those of us that employ some of these techniques will probably have some issues with pain that need to be addressed.

Some signs of buried pain are:

1) Disconnecting from feelings – Many people can consciously remember when they made the decision to disconnect. It will usually be in child-hood or adolescence. They experience immediate relief from this withdrawal and this is usually enough to prevent them from reconnecting. When we disconnect from feelings, we usually block out **ALL** feeling. We are therefore unable to feel joy, happiness or love. This can often create problems in relationships.

2) Insensitivity to the feelings of others – If we are not in touch with our own feelings there may be a tendency to forget what pain is like. Consequently

we may inflict hurt on other people without having any notion of what we are doing to them. This pattern is often found in the family arena.

3) Workaholism – When we are busy working and this takes up 100% of our attention, there is no time to think or feel. Many people who choose to work long hours dread weekends or holidays. They do not have their work to hide behind. These people do not make good romantic partners or parents as both of these areas of life involve time and feelings.

4) Keeping busy – This is an extension of the workaholic. These people never sit down and relax, they have to have something to **DO** all the time. It may be hobbies or jobs around the house. They have a restless energy and may find it difficult to even sit down to a meal. There is a belief that it is hard to hit a moving target. If we cannot pin some-one down then they will be protected from having their pain triggered by people and situations.

5) Spending time with inanimate objects rather than people – People tend to bring up our baggage, so we

may watch television, play computer games or log onto the Internet. This gives the illusion of interacting with others and yet they are not going to tap into our feelings or give us "grief".

6)   Needing to hurt others – This is a classic sign of unresolved hurt. We are afraid of getting hurt so we make sure we hurt others first. This pattern often emerges within relationships and will be very destructive.

7)   Bullying or controlling – This is an extension of needing to hurt others. Virtually all bullies will have been bullied or controlled. There will be considerable pain around this. They will have been made to feel powerless. Their method of dealing with this is to assume power over someone else and render them powerless. Bullies take pleasure in their actions and do not empathise with their victims in any way.

8)   Not being able to find a relationship – If we are not in a relationship and want to be, it is usually because our fear of getting hurt outweighs our desire to get our needs met. We will have been hurt in the past either in a previous relationship or in

childhood and we unconsciously protect ourselves from being hurt again. However this does not work. We will end up feeling hurt that no one appears to want us or we will experience a great deal of loneliness due to our withdrawal.

9) Hiding behind anger – Many angry people are simply using their anger to protect them from feeling their hurt. They have a vested interest in not releasing their anger as they would lose the buffer zone to their pain. These people often view their pain as being vulnerable and weak. They would rather be unpopular for their aggression than risk experiencing their hurt.

10) Finding it difficult to commit – When we choose to live our lives on a shallow superficial level there is often an issue with hurt. We do not allow people to get too close to us either in friendships or relationships. The belief is that if we do not invest too much in them then they will not be able to hurt us. These people will often withdraw or move on at the point where there is any intimacy.

11) Victim mentality – Victims will carry their hurt

and pain around with them and wear it like a coat. This will create a very uncomfortable mirror for anyone who is trying to suppress their pain. Victims will often attract attack from these people. Very often victims will not want to release their pain. They wear it like a medal of honour and may think that they get attention and sympathy from being hurt.

12) Using substances – Many people turn to drink, drugs or cigarettes to keep their pain at bay. This may seem to be effective in the short term but will ultimately create a great deal more pain in themselves and others than they are trying to guard against.

Virtually all these methods we have of dealing with pain are designed so that we do not have to feel the pain. However in most of these scenarios we end up creating more pain or situations in life that are even more detrimental. Instead of wasting valuable energy in building up protection mechanisms that do not work anyway, we could simply decide to access the pain and let it go.

FEAR AND HURT

Our fear of being hurt governs much of our behaviour in life. At the root of most of our fears is a belief that we will be hurt either emotionally or physically. It has to be said that many people can cope with physical pain much better than emotional. This is because the body has a natural healing mechanism that will deal with the physical. It may seem as if we are destined to live with our emotional pain forever.

When we have a fear it is because we have experienced the situation in the past and we know how painful it was at the time and we dread the possibility of it happening again.

We are so powerful that whatever we focus our attention on, we can end up creating. We have a tendency to create and attract the very things that we are afraid of.

We will only be free from fear and pain at the point that we acknowledge that these things are an illusion. We are always afraid of something that may or may not happen in the **FUTURE**. In this actual moment there is no cause for fear. Even when we are in a difficult situation, we do not feel fear until after the danger has past. We are focusing all our energy and attention into dealing with the emergency.

If we have a fear, at the point where it actually happens we do not feel fear, we most likely feel pain. For instance, if we fear abandonment and we are in a relationship, we may dread the day when our partner dumps or leaves us. If this eventually happens, we do not fear it but we feel the pain that it has triggered. We will experience again the feelings that we felt when we have been abandoned in the past. Fear is always an illusion because the thing that we are afraid of has not yet happened so it does not **EXIST**.

We can choose how we think and feel about a situation. Given the same situation we can create a win for ourselves. We are in a relationship and we accept that we will remain in this union until it no longer serves us. If the relationship is not working then it is a blessing that both sides are free to find happiness else where.

Our fear of being hurt will affect most areas of life, the predominant ones being relationships, the family and the work place. If our fear is very strong, then we will severely limit ourselves. We will make sure that we do not put ourselves in situations where we could possibly be hurt. We might even get to the point of seeing potential for hurt in even the most innocuous places and remove ourselves from them altogether.

HURT IS ALWAYS AN ILLUSION. WHEN WE CHOOSE TO BE HURT, WE CREATE THAT REALITY

HURT AND ANGER

Hurt and anger are two emotions that are very closely linked. It is quite common to feel both of these emotions at the same time. However, many of us have different responses to these feelings. Some of us are able to express and feel our pain but see anger as being unacceptable. This is often a female trait. On the other hand there are many men who do not want to feel their hurt but they have no problem with anger as it may seem like a macho emotion. Having said this there are many people who do not like to experience either of these feelings.

We often use our anger to protect us from being hurt but as with most defence mechanisms, this does not work. It usually ends up creating the very situation that it is there to guard against. When we are angry, we usually upset or make others angry. They then look for ways to get back at us for affecting them in this way. We then end up being hurt and rejected by them.

Ultimately our aim is to release and remove all our anger and hurt. We may have to tackle the anger first in order to get access to the pain. There are many people who create a very tough prickly facade. This is usually to disguise and protect a great deal of hurt, which has been created in childhood. We may find it very difficult to get near them. Their fear of being hurt is so great that they keep people away from them. Once again this ploy is counter-productive. We may think that they are the tough, hard people they are trying to portray and conse-quently we are equally tough in our dealings with them. This then reinforces their need to protect themselves and so the cycle goes on. If these peo-ple released the pain that they are protecting, they could then dismantle the facade and attract people and situations that are much more gentle and giving.

It is important to acknowledge the part that anger plays in the creation of our pain. It is quite natural that we would be angry with people who have hurt us in the past.

HURT AND JOY

Every feeling can either be positive or negative. It depends on the charge that we put on it. Sadness is the negative charge of this feeling and joy is the positive.

If we look at the physiological response to this feeling, we experience a welling up of emotion, we may get a lump in the throat and then tears appear and fall. This is how we respond when we are upset. However when we are overcome with happiness, we have the exact same feelings. This can happen in many different circumstances for example, when we see a beautiful sunset or when we give and receive love.

When we suppress our hurt, we are depriving ourselves of experiencing the wonderful feelings of joy, ecstasy, bliss and happiness. We are aware that we can enjoy having a good cry. Why else do we choose to watch weepy films again and again?

Our ultimate goal is to release all our stored up pain and sadness and this will enable us to feel joy and happiness as our natural and constant state.

HURT AND PROTECTION

When we have a great deal of hurt, we will employ techniques to protect ourselves from feeling the pain. However, most methods that we use fail abysmally. We will look at some of the ways we may unconsciously use to protect ourselves.

1)   Anger – We have just seen that many people who appear to be aggressive, testy or stroppy are using these things as a smoke screen for their pain. We have also seen that we end up being hurt if we use this method.

2)   Shyness and withdrawal – When we have been hurt in the past, we may well withdraw and become shy of people and situations that involve interacting with others. We have all seen children who put themselves on the edge of their peer group because they are afraid of being rejected and therefore hurt. This particular ploy does not work.

Shyness is often seen as arrogance and that we believe ourselves too good to mix with ordinary folk. We therefore still feel rejected and hurt.

3)   Strength and independence – Most of our hurt is created out of not getting what we need and want from other people. A very effective means of protection is to make sure that we don't need anyone. The downside of this particular technique is that we may end up being lonely and isolated from our fellow human beings. Also, when we deny others an opportunity to give to us, it may appear to them that we have rejected them. We may end up creating the same feeling in others that we are seeking to avoid in ourselves.

4)   Eccentricity – With eccentricity, we are in effect removing ourselves from the arena of normal life. Here we cannot be hurt or rejected if we are the ones that have rejected everyone else. When we are eccentric, no one expects or demands anything from us. We can therefore live in our own little world without interference.

5)   Self-effacement – This technique involves putting ourselves down before others can. For instance, we might always refer to ourselves as being stupid or ugly or having big ears. This then means that other people either try and refute this assessment or refrain from referring to it. We believe that it is better for people to laugh with us rather than at us. If we are all laughing at the big ears, then we can cope. If other people are laughing at us, then it hurts. Within this method we are in danger of creating very low self-esteem. When we are constantly belittling ourselves we will end up believing our own negative propaganda.

6)   Disconnecting from feelings – The belief is that if we do not experience our feelings then we cannot be hurt by other people. However, if we cut off from our feelings, we have to make sure we don't put ourselves in a position to have feelings brought up. We must do work that only involves the mind and logic. We cannot pursue creative pastimes since this puts us in touch with the part of the brain that also assimilates feelings. Relationships will

usually trigger our feelings so we will either avoid them altogether or we get into them and end up being hurt because our partner cannot handle our cold attitude. When we cut off from hurt we also cut off from love.

It is important to notice whether we use a technique to protect from feeling hurt. If so, does this work for us or against us? If it is the latter, then we may as well dismantle this mode of behaviour and look for other solutions.

HURT AND DEFENSIVENESS

We have already seen the techniques that can be employed to protect us from being hurt. There is however, a pattern of protection that is responsible for most of the pain and destructive behaviour in the world. This is defensiveness.

When we use this particular mode of being, it is because we feel that the best form of defence is attack, or get them before they get you. This particular ploy **NEVER** works because when we defend we invite attack. This pattern usually runs something like this. We have been hurt in the past and we were made to feel powerless in this situation. We then decide that the only way not to feel hurt in future is to be the one that inflicts the pain on others. We then go out and look for people to hurt, usually choosing those who are vulnerable or have some quality or gift that makes us feel uncomfortable. When we have done or said something that has hurt that person, they will either do or say something to hurt us back or they will remove their love, respect or approval in which case we lose anyway.

This pattern appears in many areas of life. In the family or sibling rivalry, in schools with bullying, in relationships, in the workplace or with despotic world leaders. If we look at the rise and fall of Hitler, we can see the whole of this pattern playing out. This is obviously an extreme case but it probably caused more pain and sadness than any situation in our modern history. All this due to one hurt little man using defensiveness as a means of dealing with his pain. Sixty years later we are still dealing with the aftermath.

It is important that we look at the situation from the opposite viewpoint. Every time someone appears to attack us or does or says something hurtful, instead of choosing to be hurt or being defensive in return, we can see that they are coming from a position of hurt and powerlessness. If we acknowledge this we can react with compassion for the cause of the other person's pain at the same time not allowing ourselves to be rendered powerless by it.

A PERSON ONLY EVER DOES SOMETHING HURTFUL FROM A POSITION OF HURT, FEAR OR IGNORANCE.

If this understanding is brought into the consciousness of mankind and acted upon, then we could eliminate most of the hurt that is generated on this earth.

HURT AND RELATIONSHIPS

Relationships are probably the one area of life that is almost guaranteed to bring our pain and sadness to our attention. Consequently they also create a wonderful opportunity to let it go and be free to relate unhindered by our fear of pain.

When we are not in a relationship it is usually because our fear of being hurt outweighs our desire to get our needs met. This is usually an unconscious process. We will have been hurt in the past. We may even perceive that relationships are synonymous with being hurt and so we shut down this side of ourselves.

In relationships we tend to recreate situations and patterns from childhood. We may even cast our partner in the role of one or both of our parents. Inevitably, virtually all of our unhealed pain and damage from childhood will emerge. However, we will probably have lost sight of the fact that it is actually about our childhood and we will then project the baggage onto our partner. At the same time they might be doing a similar thing to us.

We will also have an unrealistic expectation that our partners give us and make up for all the things we didn't get that we needed as a child. When they are unable or unwilling to do this we will often feel hurt or think that they do not love us anymore.

We are living in times when more relationships break up than survive. It is rare to come across a broken relationship that has not manifested a huge amount of hurt. This is not just for the participants but to any children involved as well. In highly evolved societies, there is an understanding that a relationship only lasts while the two people involved are compatible. If one grows or moves quicker than the other or if they go in different directions, their energy is no longer in harmony. They move on without blame or acrimony and hurt does not play a part in this equation. This is an ideal that we could grow towards. While we see a relationship as a life long commitment and that we have failed when it does not work long term, then we are going to be stuck in the destructive cycle of hurt and blame.

It is very common in relationships to take on hurt where none is intended. We are always looking for signs that our partner's love for us is waning.

Consequently, we will always find them. When we choose to feel hurt, we will often look for ways to hurt them back. In a relationship we are privy to intimate information about our partner and we will often use this as a means of hurting them. They will then either withdraw or look for ways to hurt us back. When this pattern is in place, it is very difficult to get back to the initial misunderstanding or unintended slight and sort it out. Communication is essential if the healing is to take place.

A successful relationship is dependent on our being **OPEN** and sharing the innermost core part of ourselves with our partner. In the early stages of a relationship this will often be the case. We are "in love" and we think that this state will last for ever. However as the relationship progresses and our patterns and damage from the past begin to emerge, things start to change. As soon as our partner begins to say and do things that are hurtful, then we begin to shut down. We do not allow them access to our innermost thoughts and feelings and the love starts to diminish. It is essential that we work through the hurt that emerges in the relationship, instead of blaming our partner and then shutting them out.

A great deal of our hurt in childhood is caused by not getting our needs and desires met. We have an unconscious expectation that our life partner fulfils these needs. This is an impossible task and with the best will in the world they will always fall short of our demands. When we perceive that we are not getting our needs met, we will feel hurt and project this onto our partner and then stop meeting some of their needs in return. To heal this particular pattern we need to be aware that our needs are simply things that we did not receive in childhood. We can fulfil our own needs or choose to perceive that we already have anything we want. When we do this, we remove a huge burden and expectation from our other half that they could not possibly fulfil. We also remove the inevitable hurt we feel when they fail us.

It is important to dissociate the hurt that comes up from our partner. We can then discover where it is from and what we need to learn about it. We can then release and heal it without causing any damage to the relationship. When we work this way, each time hurt surfaces, it can be a wonderful opportunity and not another nail in the coffin of the relationship.

SADNESS AND LOSS

Most pain and sadness is created out of a sense of loss. Sometimes we will perceive a loss of love, support, attention, approval or care. There are many life changing events that are guaranteed to bring up hurt. Death and the break up of a relationship are the two strongest. In both these cases there is a sense of physical separation as well as the inevitable emotional loss.

We have a well of pain inside us where all our unexpressed and unhealed hurt is stored. Various triggers will bring a certain amount of this pain to the surface. If this is not released when it comes up, then it will return to the well and be re-triggered at a later date. When we experience the death of a loved one, the pain is often so strong that a vast proportion of our stored sadness will come up. This may be so overwhelming that we become engulfed in our grief and we cannot see a way out of it.

I have often come across cases in my practice where a client has lost a parent and they have been estranged or were not close. They are amazed at the amount of grief that came up. What happens here is that we re-experience the pain in childhood from when we were first abandoned whether emotionally or physically. This hurt may well have been buried or suppressed from the point where it was first created. The death and resulting bereavement offer a marvellous opportunity to heal and release the original wound.

When we lose a loved one, grief is a normal part of the bereavement process. We usually experience the whole gamut of negative emotions. Anger, guilt and sadness all have a part to play and we have to work through each feeling in order to come through the process and to be able to return to some semblance of normality.

The ideal way to deal with grief from a loss or bereavement is to allow the feeling to surface and then to express it so that it does not have to play a part in our lives any further. However, there are two ways that some people inappropriately deal with grief. Neither of these is very healthy.

Firstly, we have seen that some people go to extraordinary lengths in order not to feel their pain. They might detach from their feelings or try to keep busy all the time. (See list of ways of protecting from the pain.) When we defer our grieving by employing these techniques, we will only have to deal with them at a later date. The body may even have some sort of breakdown in order for us to do our grieving. This method can also cause untold damage to the physical body.

The second inappropriate way of dealing with the grief is to allow it to surface without making any moves to release, heal or express it. The pain does not go anywhere, we wallow in it and may even use it to punish ourselves with. We find it very difficult to function in our lives. We might also wear out the sympathy and patience of those around us, who may end up deserting us. There are many people who choose to remain stuck for the rest of their lives. We may have the misguided idea that we owe this amount of sadness to the one who has died. To be happy would be a betrayal or disrespectful to their memory. The opposite of this is in fact true.

When we can acknowledge that death is a cause for celebration and not despair, we will be free of the detrimental legacy of bereavement. One of the laws of the Universe is that energy can neither be created or destroyed, it simply changes form. When someone dies the essence of who they are simply changes form. The form that they become is actually more accessible to us since it is not working with the limitations of the physical body and the ego mind. Far from losing a loved one we are gaining their love and support in a much more powerful form. I often think that this process is probably very similar to how it must have been in the old days when a family member emigrated. They are going to a better life with more opportunity. The family are happy for them but are aware that they will miss them on a physical level. However, they are still able to connect and communicate.

BEREAVEMENT AND PETS

We often find that we are able to open up and relate to animals far more easily than we can to humans. We perceive that animals give us unconditional love and accept us just as we are. They do not do things that hurt us, instead they keep on giving through thick and thin. However, the one area where animals do cause us pain is when they die. We may grieve our dead pets far more acutely than we do our relatives.

I believe that the animal kingdom is very well attuned to us. In my experience when a well loved pet dies, it usually does so at a time that is very significant for us. Sometimes it happens so that we can move on to pastures new unencumbered. Other times the death will often be a part of a big healing process. Our unhealed pain is triggered and brought to the surface in order that we release it and remove its detrimental effect from the body. It is important to realise this and not to allow this wonderful opportunity to go to waste. We do not want to compound and add to our well of pain with our grief, we want to use it to access and empty the well of hurt.

I have come across many cases where people have experienced so much pain at the loss of a pet that they vow not to have another. They couldn't bear to feel this pain again. Alternatively they do not allow themselves to get too close to or fond of an animal.

For many children the loss of a pet is the first experience they have with death. This may occur at a time when they are very vulnerable and emotional. It may also lead them to conclude that eventually everyone they love and need is going to die and leave them. This may create a huge sense of insecurity if the whole incident is not handled carefully.

We often end up dealing with our grief over the loss of our human relatives and friends through the death of our animals. Our pain and grief is not compartmentalised. To some extent it is all lumped in together. This is why a supposedly small incident can trigger a disproportional amount of hurt. We can take advantage of this situation by letting it go.

PLEASURE AND PAIN

One of our main objectives in life is to learn, grow and expand our consciousness. For the most part, we go through life unaware and half asleep. We get so caught up in survival and the minutiae of living that we no longer see the big picture and the part we play in it.

Due to our degree of unconsciousness, it may take quite a lot to get our attention, in order to learn the lessons and to adjust our perspective to a way that serves us. Sometimes we are faced with something that is so big that we cannot ignore it. We will then take stock and look at what is important and make the changes in our lives. I have heard countless people say that a life threatening illness, redundancy or bankruptcy was the best thing that could have happened to them because it was a catalyst for making changes that have resulted in them being a better, happier person. There are many other people who fail to heed the wake up call and allow these things to create more pain and struggle and the opportunity is wasted.

We are coming into a time where we can learn our lessons through pleasure and not pain. The most important aspect of this is that we be awake and conscious of what lessons are being presented to us. In my experience, if something happens more than once then there is usually a message or lesson attached to the incident. We then need to use our powers of detection to discover exactly what the message is. There is no such thing as coincidence, so when we encounter what appears to be one, there is usually some deeper significance attached to it. Finding the lessons can be a part of the pleasure that we experience. Once we are on this path and are open to learning and growing, every time we experience pain, it is because it is there for release.

HURT AND
POWERLESSNESS

We have already seen that virtually all pain we experience is either due to a sense of loss or not getting our needs met. Most of this pain comes from the child aspect of ourselves. It is in childhood that we are most needy. We are dependent on other people for our very existence. This then gives us a sense of being powerless to meet our own needs and desires. When we grow up, we find that we are still powerless to meet any needs that were consistently not met as a child. This is an illusion but we keep on trying to get other people to give us what we need and we are hurt when they inevitably do not.

We take our power back into our own hands when we choose to perceive that **WE ALREADY HAVE EVERYTHING THAT WE NEED OR WANT**. We become powerless when we are reliant on another for what we want. We do not have power over anyone other than ourselves. However, we have so much power available to us. One of the most powerful aspects of ourselves is the ability to **CREATE** everything that we think, feel and believe. If we then believe that we have **EVERYTHING** that we need and want, then this is exactly what we create. The sources of our needs and wants are many and varied and we will not know where they are coming from until they arrive. This takes the expectation and pressure off any particular individual and it means that we are not hurt if and when they are not forthcoming.

One of the major truths of life is that no one may take our power, we can only give it away. Therefore, if we are feeling powerless, we need to look at who or what we have given our power to and why. There may be patterns from childhood, which are repeating and being brought to our attention in order that they be healed. Just as we consciously or unconsciously give our power away, we can decide to take it back. The beauty of this is that no one can touch or affect us negatively unless we **CHOOSE** to let them. We are therefore completely immune to hurt and pain.

HURT AND CONTROL

It is probably true that anyone who works with or uses control in their lives is coming from a position of hurt and pain. Often this hurt is due to having been controlled by someone else. They then perceive that the only way to deal with this is to control others. This perpetuates the cycle of abuse and hurt.

This particular pattern goes against another Universal law of life, which is **DO NOT DO UNTO OTHERS THAT WHICH YOU WOULD NOT WANT TO BE DONE UNTO YOU**. Many of us live by the opposite understanding, which is to get others before they get you, then at least we will have the upper hand. It is easy to see how destructive this can be on a global level. This is the philosophy used by bullies, despots and control freaks.

Those using control will often have disconnected from their own feelings. This means that they have lost the ability to empathise. Very often if we see people experiencing hurt from the same cause as our pain, this will then trigger our sadness. This does not happen when we use control to hurt other people. We will almost always have a sense of pleasure at witnessing their pain.

Control can be wielded in many different ways and some of them may be quite subtle. There is almost always some implied threat involved. It may be "Do what I say or I'll hurt you." or it might be "Do what I say or I won't love you or I'll leave you." A control freak will usually only choose to be around those who will allow themselves to be controlled. These people are coming from a perspective of weakness and not strength. If they are confronted by someone stronger than themselves, they will almost always crumble.

Once we are clear about the issues around control and we make a conscious decision neither to control or be controlled by others, the issue can disappear from our lives. We will not attract people to us who have a problem with control and we will be able to live and let live.

HURT, JUDGEMENT AND CRITICISM

THE NEED IN OTHERS TO JUDGE AND CRITICISE IS DUE TO A SENSE OF THEIR OWN INADEQUACY AND NOT OURS.

Being judged or criticised generates a huge amount of pain. We may go out of our way to avoid situations where we might be criticised. When we are judged, we are made to feel small and not good enough.

One of the most freeing things we can do for ourselves is to **GENUINELY** not care what other people think of us. When this occurs, we will find that we do not attract people into our lives that will judge us.

It is very important to remind ourselves that what other people think of us is none of our business. It is always a reflection of them and their feelings about themselves, which they then project onto us. Children have a way of saying it. "Twinkle, twinkle little star, what you say is what you are."

This is a very accurate assessment. We will often notice that people who are very judgmental will go around accusing other people of the very things that they do or are.

It is also very easy to get self-righteous about our criticism and believe that we are helping to improve that person by telling them exactly what is wrong with them. The fact is that the only helpful criticism is **NO** criticism. I have often noticed that the people who are most prone to giving out criticism are the least able to take it. Once again, it is a defence mechanism.

We want to reach a point where we do not experience any hurt, even when those around us offer judgements and criticism. To do this we need to be conscious that anything negative that comes out of their mouths is nothing to do with us but is showing how little they think of themselves. When this understanding is in place we need never be hurt in this way again.

Equally we need to become aware of our own need to judge and criticise others. The ego will be at the root of all judgements that we make. The ego will constantly tell us that we are not good enough and then it will look around to find things about other people to judge, in order that we feel better about ourselves. We will often have the need to judge those that we perceive are, do or have more than us. We are trying to bring them down to size so that we do not feel so inadequate in comparison to them. This pattern is particularly prevalent in the ego based media. As soon as someone rises up out of the ranks, they will be shot down so that we do not feel that they are better than us.

The fact is that we only ever see in others, qualities that we actually have ourselves. Everything we judge others for, we will also have an awareness of in ourselves. How else would we be able to see it? The bible uses the example of pointing out the splinter in someone else's eye, while ignoring the plank in our own. We can also be aware of the positive aspect of this, which is that everything we admire or compliment others for, we actually have ourselves.

HURT AND PHYSICAL PAIN

When we studiously refuse to deal with and heal the emotional pain that we have stored and suppressed in the body, it will have to find somewhere to go. Unexpressed emotional pain may become physical pain.

Pain is only ever there to show us something that is unhealed. It is a messenger that is trying to get our attention. Once it has got through to us and we have acted on the information that it is there to provide, then the pain has no reason to remain.

It is no coincidence that we use the same words to describe the physical and emotional feeling since they are so closely linked. If we are trying to deal with our physical ailments, it would be very remiss to ignore the emotional side of the issue.

There are obviously some conditions that are more likely to be affected by the suppression of pain and sadness than others. We are aware of the phrase, "dying of a broken heart". The heart is the centre of our love and security and when these two areas are compromised we will experience a great deal of hurt and this will affect us. Tumours, cysts and diabetes may also be fed by our pain.

Many ailments that are very physically painful like back problems and arthritis can be relieved by the expression of emotions, particularly hurt.

There are some people who choose to mutilate themselves. They will use razors or broken glass to cut themselves. These people are usually in so much emotional pain that they are desperate for some way to alleviate it. They find that if they do something to hurt themselves, the hurt transfers from the emotional to the physical and this is by far the lesser of two evils. They experience immense relief from the pain and sadness as a result. To many people this behaviour would seem to be crazy but it is actually very logical to the sufferer. These people have usually experienced traumas or abuse in childhood and are trying to deal with the residual pain.

It is a great shame that dealing with emotions is not part of our medical programs. A huge amount of money could be saved from drugs and surgery if emotional clearing were implemented.

THE "POOR ME" SYNDROME

When we have a victim mentality, we will constantly be aware of our hurt and what has been "done" to us in the past. A victim is usually very passive and completely unaware of how he or she has created and attracted certain life situations.

To a victim the pain and sorrow that have been created by circumstances and people around them are the scars that they proudly display to the world to show the degree to which they have suffered. They have a vested interest in not letting this pain go or they would have nothing to show for their experiences.

When we are in victim mode, most of our pain is on the surface. We have no reason to suppress our hurt. We may get a great deal of attention or sympathy for our pain. We might even be known by other people as "poor...". We tend to wear out the sympathy of those around us when we are in "poor me" mode and will consequently have to keep on finding new friends and acquaintances to feel sorry for us.

It is generally acknowledged that the best release of sadness is by crying. However, when we are feeling sorry for ourselves, we may be constantly crying but there is no reduction in the amount of pain. It is as if the tears recycle themselves back into us. Victims are often so busy being sorry for themselves that they are not aware of other people's pain or the fact that they are hurting their family with their pain and the unwillingness to let it go and lead a joyful, fulfilling life.

THE SPECTRUM OF HURT

There is a huge spectrum of hurt that we can experience. Some forms of pain are quite mild while others threaten to overwhelm us.

At the lower end of the scale we have sadness, upset, misery or unhappiness. At the other end of the spectrum we have grief, despair and desolation. The level of pain we experience will decide the depth to which we go into our well of pain and the amount of hurt that comes up to the surface. We can see from this that the situations that bring up the most pain also offer the greatest opportunity for release.

There is nothing that happens to us in life that is not ultimately for our highest good. This includes all the negative and life changing things that happen to us. These are either there to show patterns of behaviour that do not work or serve us or give us the opportunity to heal old outdated feelings and beliefs. It is important that we embrace any situation that brings our pain to the surface and to do the necessary release.

HURT AND FORGIVENESS

Pain and anger will almost always be aimed at a person rather than a situation. An essential part of the healing process is therefore to forgive the person that we perceived to have caused the hurt in the first place. To a certain extent this can only happen when we have released the hurt and anger surrounding them.

In order to forgive someone we have to change our perception and understanding of the situations that have created our hurt. This can immediately lift any negative charge that we put onto them at the time of creation. Once this is done it is any easy process to instate forgiveness. When we do this we change the relationship we have with this person for the better. It is important to note that this needs to happen even if the person has died or we are no longer in touch with them.

Forgiveness frees us up from experiencing and carrying around the heavy negative emotions from the past. We want to have a clean slate so that we can consciously create the rest of our lives unhindered by old negative patterns and grievances.

FORGIVENESS
HEALS
ALL

PART II

DEALING WITH

AND

RELEASING

HURT AND

SADNESS

DEALING WITH HURT

In removing pain and sadness from our lives, we need to approach it from two different angles. Firstly, we want to release the pain that is stored in the body and that we are suppressing. We also want to remove the triggers that allow us to re-experience and add to the well of hurt inside. Secondly, we want to change how we view the world so that we need never feel any pain, hurt or sadness again. Taking this even further, we also want to ensure that we do not consciously or unconsciously inflict pain on others due to our words or actions. If enough people were to make this a natural way of being, then the domino effect of this can begin to eliminate hurt and pain from the face of the Earth.

The only way this can happen is if we have first removed it from our inner and outer world and teach others by our example to do the same. Obviously this is not something that will happen overnight, it is a gradual process that starts with the willingness to release our own pain.

At the end of the day, we may feel like individuals but we are part of a great whole. Just as we have our own consciousness, we are also part of a group consciousness and every change we make in ourselves will have some effect on the group energy. We have talked of the well of pain that is within us and this is also contained within the group consciousness. Never has this been more clearly demonstrated than with the death of Princess Diana. All over the world, millions of people tapped into the mass pain and made huge inroads into releasing it by their displays of grief. People who never normally cried or allowed themselves to feel hurt were unable to protect themselves from feeling and expressing their pain. Diana was simply the catalyst for this and she performed the role she was here to do.

We will look at the means by which we can move along the path to eliminating pain and hurt from ourselves and the world as a whole.

POSITIONS OF HURT

Our hurt and pain will be in one of three positions: suppressed, on the surface or expressed.

When our hurt is suppressed we may not even be aware of its existence. This is particularly true when we employ some of the techniques of protection and defensiveness. Some people may be very aware of the amount of hurt they have inside and go around in a perpetual state of fear that it will be triggered. Our hurt is usually housed in the solar plexus area of the body. We feel very vulnerable in this area and we may go to great lengths to protect it. Sometimes we put on weight in order to provide some padding over the solar plexus. The most common way in which we protect the solar plexus is with our arms. Whenever we feel vulnerable and fear being hurt, we fold our arms or hold them across the solar plexus. This in effect shuts people out so that they won't cause us pain.

I do not think there is a single person in this world that has not got some hurt and pain suppressed in the body. The more unfeeling or heartless we seem to be, the more pain we probably have inside. When our hurt is in the suppressed position, it will either be doing damage to the body or it will always be threatening to surface and therefore come to our conscious attention.

The next position for pain to be is on the surface. This is a **VERY** uncomfortable place for it to be. We will feel upset and possibly in tears. Something will have come along to trigger our pain and bring it to the surface. At this point various mechanisms come into play to try to stop us from having the pain and to push it back down to the suppressed position. The first thing that happens is that our throat closes up. This creates the feeling of a lump in the throat. We then go into a swallowing reflex, as if to swallow the lump and prevent the feeling from coming up still further. If we are not successful, then tears will start to gather in the eyes. We then click in with the sobbing mechanism which is also designed to push the hurt back down. We can see that when we sob, we are taking the breath right down to the solar plexus which gives a little jerk each time. **HOWEVER**, in this mode, we keep on taking the breath in without letting any significant amount of breath **OUT**. This is the very thing that will let the hurt go. We often find that we sob until we are exhausted or the feeling has subsided (gone back down). This may give us the **ILLUSION** of having expressed our pain but it is still there to emerge on another occasion.

EXPRESSION is the only way we have of releasing our hurt and pain. This involves allowing ourselves to feel the emotion on the surface and then letting it go and removing it from the body altogether. We might well wish that we had a magic wand that would take all our pain away without our having to connect with it. Hurt is a feeling and we can only release a feeling by feeling it. However, the good news is that we do not have to experience it for more than a few moments before we can let it go and once this is done, it need never play a part in our lives again. In this process we have to change many deep seated patterns and beliefs that are given to us by society as well as our own personal experience. The rewards for doing this are immense.

THE PROCESS FOR REMOVING PAIN

There are certain steps that we need to be aware of and work through if we are to remove pain from our lives.

1) We need to have a willingness to do the necessary stages to release our pain. If this is not there or is only half hearted, then we will not progress any further.

2) Put out the intention of removing all pain and sadness from your life. This sets in motion a whole unseen network of help, guidance and support to bring about this end.

3) Commit to the process.

4) Look at the particular mechanisms that you employ in order not to feel or express pain. (See protection chapter.)

5) Begin to dismantle these structures by

becoming aware of when you use them and **CHOOSING** to act differently each time they emerge.

6)   When hurt or pain surfaces, welcome it and see it as a wonderful opportunity for **RELEASE**.

7)   Do the releasing process as soon as possible after it has surfaced.

8)   When the feeling has gone, look at what has triggered the hurt. This will be a pattern or issue that we have that needs to be healed and removed.

9)   Put the trigger into a cohesive statement.

10)   Do the process for finding and releasing the source of pain.

11)   When we find ourselves in a situation that could allow us to be hurt, instate the necessary understanding in order not to feel the pain.

I will go through these points in more detail, giving techniques to help with each step of the process.

WILLINGNESS, INTENTION AND COMMITMENT

These three qualities are so important because without them it is very difficult to make anything other than superficial changes in our lives.

We also need to be aware whether we actually want to release and remove our hurt and pain from our lives. There may well be a payoff for hanging onto it. This will vary with different people. There are two common reasons for holding onto our hurt. Firstly, we may want to punish the person or people we perceive to have created it. If they see us looking miserable or unable to thrive in our lives, then the resulting guilt will in some way compensate us for our hurt. Secondly, we may get attention and sympathy for our pain and sadness and think that if we no longer had it, people would ignore us or abandon us. The fact is that when we are happy, we attract people to us like magnets. We would all rather be with a happy person than a miserable one.

Our **WILL** is very strong and it is important that we align it with what we want in life and what will serve us at the highest level. Our will is a key aspect of helping us to survive in childhood. We may develop a rebellious streak as a defence against abuse or control. While this might serve us when we are young, it may not do so as an adult. We become the ones that we are rebelling against. Every time we put forward a proposal of change, we find ourselves resisting and sabotaging it.

INTENTION is a very powerful mechanism. When we clearly form an intention, we activate a process, both internal and external that presents us with what we need to manifest our intention. The opportunities will be given to us in the perfect space and time. At first they will be presented in a gentle form but if we are not aware or awake enough to spot them, then they will arrive in a form that is guaranteed to get our attention. Sometimes this may seem to be rather drastic and is perhaps going to bring up our pain in a big way. This can obviously be avoided if we look for ways to deal with our pain. For instance, I was in a supermarket car park and I saw a lady with a laden trolley waiting to cross the road. I stopped the car and indicated to her that she could go. She gave me an impatient look and waved me on. I felt devastated and rejected and nearly cried. This response was totally out of proportion to the situation. I realised that this was an opportunity to release my pain with an incident that was essentially trivial and did not threaten my stability in any way.

COMMITMENT is to the process. It has to be said that once this is underway, we cannot just stop it. Our issues around hurt will continue to arise and if we do not continue to process them when they surface, then we will remain stuck in the feeling quite needlessly. It is also important to point out that it need only take a few minutes to process, if we have the commitment to do so.

RELEASING PAIN

Once pain comes to the surface, we are able to deal with it and let it go. Consequently we need to welcome and embrace it, when it comes to our attention, Instead of doing the natural thing, which is to try and push it back down again. When pain emerges, there are two things we need to do. Firstly, to release the feeling and then to find and clear the source of it. When we do this we will not have to feel pain for that particular issue ever again.

BREATHING

The most effective means of releasing pain is with the breath. It not only connects us with the hurt in the body but it also lets it go. Many people breathe very shallowly in order not to connect with their feelings. The solar plexus is the centre of emotion in the body. By allowing the breath to reach this part we can access some of our deep emotion.

When we access pain we are likely to breathe in to try to push the feelings back down into the body. However the release of it is dependent on the **OUT** breath. This needs to be done with force, so that we can hear the breath being released. We then continue to do this until the feelings of pain are no longer there.

To recap:

1)   When hurt surfaces, deepen the breath.
2)   Access the pain by taking the breath to the place where it is in the body.
3)   Expel the air with the pain attached, forcefully from the body.
4)   Repeat this until you can no longer feel the pain in the solar plexus.
5)   The breath will come out smoothly and gently.
6)   Have a sense of peace and calm in the area where the pain was a few moments ago.

CRYING

Crying is a very good form of expression of pain and if used in conjunction with the breathing technique can be very powerful.

There is a substance within tears that is very healing. However, it is not there when we cry with joy or if our eyes water in the wind. When we access our pain and cry, we activate the natural healing mechanism in the body.

We are often embarrassed about shedding tears around other people. We may not comfortable with other people crying in front of us. We want them to stop, so we try and distract them or make them laugh, when in fact we should encourage them to cry the sadness out of the body. Every time this does not happen, we have missed a wonderful opportunity to release some of our pain.

There are some tears which do not release our pain but instead seem to recycle it. These are what I call "poor me" tears. Every time we choose to perceive ourselves as victims, we perpetuate our pain and sadness. The tears are there to say "Look at the terrible things that have been done to me." They are often there also to invoke the sympathy of others.

1) When tears come up, welcome them.
2) Remove yourself from anyone who is likely to try and stop you from crying.
3) Allow the tears to flow freely.
4) Use the breath to expel the feeling.
5) Keep the process going until there are no more tears.

FINDING THE TRIGGER

We will all have many different things that bring up our pain. These will vary from person to person, depending on our past experiences and issues. Each time we find ourselves in a situation that recreates any aspect of the original cause, our hurt will surface. We can see that we can use the techniques to release the pain when it arises but this will not prevent it from returning the next time we experience that particular trigger. If we want to eliminate pain from our lives, we will have to remove the things that created it in the first place.

The first stage of this process is to recognise the triggers that bring up our hurt. Usually we are so busy reacting to the situation that we are unaware of what is going on. Common triggers for hurt are rejection, loss, criticism, indifference, lack of acknowledgement or consideration and the anger of others.

1) When your pain comes to your attention, take a few moments to work out what is going on.

2) Who is the person that triggered it?

3) What was said or done or not said or done, to bring up your hurt?

4) What did you feel and think as a result of this?

5) Put this into a cohesive statement linking all the different parts. For instance, when my boyfriend does not phone or turn up when he says he is going to, I feel rejected and as if I do not matter to him and this hurts.

6) Take note as to whether these feelings have been brought up in the past in similar circumstances.

FINDING THE SOURCE

Once we have identified the triggers for our pain, we can move onto the next stage of the process, which is to find and clear the source. Obviously there will be a different source for all the various causes of our pain.

The source of most of our pain will be in the first few years of life and will usually relate to a sense of separation either physically or emotionally or our not getting our needs met.

There are two specific sources of pain that I am constantly having to clear with my clients. The first is the separation created when a baby is put into the hospital nursery soon after birth. At this stage, the baby does not see itself as a separate entity from its mother. Consequently, this will be as painful to the baby as losing a limb. We also need to be aware that time is a relative concept. To a new born baby, an hour is literally a lifetime and it has no way of knowing if and when it is going to be reunited with its mother. Another common scenario that I am repeatedly coming across is as follows. The baby or small child is put down for a sleep, when it awakes it cries for its mother or carer but no one comes. This can be because the mother has gone out, is asleep or cannot cope with a crying baby. The child feels abandoned and once again it has no way of knowing whether its mother is ever coming back. The feelings of abandonment will often become an ever increasing pattern in life.

If we look at these two examples, we as adults would consider them to be petty and inconsequential. We would know that in both cases that the baby was safe and taken care of. However, we need to be aware of how different a small child or baby's perception is to our own. What may be tiny to us is earth shattering to it.

The information that we need to find the source of our pain is in our unconscious mind. It is very easy to access this but we need to be aware that this will be conveyed to us through feelings and not thoughts. This is nothing that we know about, so it is useless to find it through thinking. Our feelings come through the solar plexus and simply by breathing into this area, we can find out what we need to know. If we completely surrender to this process, we will feel the feelings as we did at the time. We can then express them at source and change the perception that we took on at the time. This can then eliminate that particular pain from our lives, once and for all.

To do this process, we need to take some time when we will not be disturbed. We can either use a tape or get a friend to help in asking the questions we need. If we do this process as near to the point when the feelings have surfaced, it will be easier to access the feelings. Make sure that you are comfortable and relaxed and not distracted in any way.

1)   Use your statement of hurt that has been triggered.

2)   Ask your unconscious mind to take you back in time to the age you were when this pattern was first created. (This will usually be very small.)

3)   How old are you? Under 5? Under 3? Under 2? Under 1?

4)   Where are you? At home? At someone else's home? In a public place? The hospital?

5)   If you are at home is it inside or outside? In a living or bedroom area?

6)   Is it day time or night time?

7)   Who is there?

8)   What are you doing?

9)   What are they doing?

10)   How are you feeling?

11)   What does she/he think and believe about this situation?

12)   Where in the body is the hurt and pain sitting?

13)   Breathe into this area, let the tears appear and keep breathing forcefully on the **OUT** breath, until the feelings of pain are no longer there.

14)   Ask your unconscious mind to remove and delete this whole pattern, feelings and thoughts

from the body. (You may want to see it as a video tape. When you press the eject button, the tape comes out and you throw it away and burn it.)

15) You are now going to program in a new perception and understanding. You, as the adult, are going to explain to the little one the reality of the situation and not the illusion it has perceived. You are also going to give it the love, the security and the wisdom it needs to cope with life. Make the child feel good about itself and to **TRUST** that everything is taken care of and that it has no need to worry.

16) When this is done and the little one feels happy and content, create a positive belief statement that can be programmed into the unconscious. This could be something like: **I GET ALL MY NEEDS AND WANTS PROVIDED IN THE PERFECT MOMENT.** OR, **I AM LOVED AND CHERISHED AT ALL TIMES.**

17) Bring these new feelings and thoughts forward in time. Take some deep breaths to anchor them in the body.

CHOOSING NOT TO HAVE HURT IN OUR LIVES

We need to be aware that hurt is always a **CHOICE** that we make. If we make this choice, we are in fact buying into an illusion that does not exist outside of our perception.

Once we remove the unconscious triggers and sources of pain, we can begin to **CONSCIOUSLY** decide how we think and feel.

Remember the following points:

1) We take on hurt when we believe that the words or actions of another person are a direct attack on us.

2) Someone only ever says or does something hurtful from a position of fear, hurt or ignorance.

3) When people are critical or judgmental, it is due to a sense of their own inadequacy and not ours.

4) What other people think of us is none of our business.

5)   If the light inside us threatens others, We do not diminish it in order to make them feel comfortable about who they are.

6)   No one can take our power, we can only give it away.

If we keep these truths in mind when we are faced with the negativity of others, then we will be able to choose to remain positive.

When we decide not to take on hurt in our lives, we will still have to deal with other people who are hell bent on defending themselves by hurting others. Here are some tips.

1)   When you are aware of hurtful words or actions coming from someone, visualise it as arrows coming towards you, that you can either step aside from or allow them to go in and hurt.

2)   In your mind, you can hold a mirror up in front of you. This is to remind you that their words are a reflection of themselves and not you.

3)   You can also use the batting technique.

Visualise a base ball bat in your hands and bat their words back to them before they touch you.

4)   Many people are so insensitive that they are unaware that they are hurting others. It may be useful to let them know in a very matter of fact way. Phrase it as a question, since this will force them to address what you have said. The one I suggest is, "Why did you say that, knowing that it is hurtful?"

5)   Bring in compassion, instead of condemning the behaviour of others and therefore adding to the negativity of the situation. This person will be coming from a state of fear or hurt. If you encountered a small child in this state, you would reassure and comfort them. This is no different. It is the small child within the fully grown adult that is displaying negativity. If you respond with love, compassion and understanding, then we can turn the tide of this extremely destructive and negative patterning.

THE EFFECTS OF RELEASING HURT

Our ultimate aim is to remove all hurt and pain from our lives. When we do this, we create a level of freedom that is hard to imagine. Our avoidance of being hurt will control and limit so many areas of life.

When we are free of pain, we create a space that can be filled with joy, fun and all the good things of life. We attract positive people and situations to us and in turn we are very generous with ourselves because we do not fear rejection or criticism for being who we are.

We can accept everything that occurs in our lives and we have no expectations for others to meet our needs or to make us happy.

Not only can we have all these things for ourselves but our example can create a knock on effect that can work towards changing the predominance of negativity in the world.

I WISH YOU A LIFE FREE FROM PAIN, HURT AND
SADNESS.

HAVE A NEW

RELEASE OF

LIFE

Also available from Diviniti Publishing Ltd.

Hypnosis tapes by Glenn Harrold.

Deep Sleep.
Complete Relaxation.
Develop Your Self Confidence.
Learn How To Think Positively.
Stop Smoking Forever.
Lose Weight Now.
Build Your Self Esteem.
Create Unlimited Financial Abundance.
Develop Successful Relationships.
Heal Your Body.
A Guided Meditation.
Develop A Powerful Memory.
Raise your Energy and Increase Motivation.
Creating Inner Peace.
Develop Your Intuition.
Overcome Fears and Phobias.
Creative Visualisation.
Learn Self Hypnosis.

Liz Adamson is available for one to one
sessions, talks and workshops.
Contact: Flat 3, Hamptons, Hadlow,
Tonbridge, Kent, TN11 9SR.
E-mail. liz@edenbook.co.uk

Available by Liz Adamson.

The Ultimate Guides To Emotions.
Releasing Anger   £4.95
Releasing Hurt and Sadness   £4.95
Embracing Love   £4.95
Embracing Happiness   £4.95

The Ultimate Guide to Relationships
                                   £7.95
The Ultimate Guide to Abundance and
Prosperity   £7.95

Contact: Diviniti Publishing Ltd.
6, Elm Walk, Aylesford, Kent ME20 7LS
Tel: 01622 792866.
E-Mail hypnosis@diviniti.co.uk